Mental Health in the Transition Phase: Coping with change

SOPHIA NEWLEAF

First published by My First Picture Book Inc. 2023

Copyright © 2023 by My First Picture Book Inc.

All rights reserved. No part of this publication may be reproduced, stored or transmitted in any form or by any means, electronic, mechanical, photocopying, recording, scanning, or otherwise without written permission from the publisher. It is illegal to copy this book, post it to a website, or distribute it by any other means without permission.

First edition

ISBN: 978-0-3696-1752-1

Contents

I Understanding Mental Health

1	Overview	3
2	Definition of Mental Health	6
3	Importance of Mental Health	9
4	Common Mental Health Disorders	12

II Mental Health During Transition Phases

5	Overview	19
6	Definition of Transition Phase	22
7	Common Transition Phases and Their Impact on Mental Health	25
8	Specific Mental Health Issues During Transition Phases	28

III Coping with Change

9	Overview	33
10	Understanding Change	37
11	The Psychological Impact of Change	40
12	Strategies for Coping with Change	44

IV Mental Health Care

13	Overview	49
14	The Role of Professional Help in Mental Health Care	52
15	Self-care Strategies for Mental Health	55
16	The Importance of Social Support in Mental Health Care	58

V Future Research Directions

17	Overview	63
18	Current Gaps in Mental Health Research	66
19	Future Research Opportunities in Mental Health	69
20	The Potential Impact of Future Mental Health Research.	73

About the Author 76

I

Understanding Mental Health

1

Overview

Mental health plays a crucial role in every phase of life, and the transition phase is a particularly sensitive period. This phase involves coping with various changes in life, such as transitioning from adolescence to adulthood, changing jobs, moving to a new city, or starting or ending relationships. The ability to navigate through these transitions and cope with the associated changes is essential for maintaining good mental health. This overview aims to provide a simple and extensive understanding of mental health in the context of the transition phase and how individuals can effectively cope with change.

Understanding Mental Health:

Mental health refers to a person's emotional, psychological, and social well-being. It affects how we think, feel, and act, and it also determines how we handle stress, relate to others, and make choices. Good mental health is vital for overall well-being and helps individuals realize their full potential, cope with the normal stresses of life, work effectively, and contribute to society.

The Transition Phase and Coping with Change:

The transition phase is a time of significant personal growth, development, and change. While change is a natural part of life, it can also be stressful and overwhelming. Coping with change effectively is crucial for maintaining mental well-being during this phase. Here are some key aspects to consider:

1. Building Resilience:

Resilience plays a vital role in coping with change. It refers to a person's ability to bounce back from challenging situations and adapt to change. Developing resilience involves building strong support networks, fostering positive coping strategies, and developing self-belief and confidence.

2. Self-awareness:

Understanding one's own strengths, weaknesses, emotions, and triggers is essential for managing change. Self-awareness helps individuals identify their personal coping mechanisms, effectively communicate their needs, and seek help when necessary.

3. Healthy Coping Strategies:

Adopting healthy coping strategies is crucial during the transition phase. This includes practicing self-care activities like exercise, maintaining a balanced diet, getting sufficient sleep, and engaging in hobbies. Additionally, seeking professional support from therapists or counselors can provide valuable guidance and tools for coping with change.

4. Social Connections:

Maintaining and nourishing healthy relationships is vital for mental well-being. Friends, family, and support groups can provide emotional support, different perspectives, and a sense of belonging during the transition phase. Building social connections also enables individuals to share experiences, gain insights, and learn from others who have gone through similar changes.

5. Setting Realistic Expectations:

Setting realistic expectations for oneself during transitional periods is important. It is essential to recognize that change takes time, and it is normal to experience ups and downs. Taking small steps, celebrating achievements, and being patient with oneself can help manage expectations and reduce unnecessary stress.

6. Seeking Professional Help:

If the challenges associated with the transition phase become overwhelming and affect daily functioning, seeking professional help is crucial. Mental health professionals can provide therapeutic interventions, guidance, and support tailored to individual needs.

Conclusion:

Understanding mental health in the context of mental health in the transition phase, particularly in coping with change, is essential for maintaining optimal well-being. Building resilience, nurturing self-awareness, adopting healthy coping strategies, fostering social connections, setting realistic expectations, and seeking professional help when needed are all key components of effectively navigating through this phase. By prioritizing mental health during times of change, individuals can embrace new experiences, manage stress, and move forward toward a fulfilling and balanced life.

2

Definition of Mental Health

Understanding mental health in the context of the subject "mental health in the transition phase: coping with change" is crucial for individuals going through significant life transitions. Mental health refers to a person's emotional, psychological, and social well-being, and it plays a vital role in how people think, feel, and behave. It also influences how individuals handle stress, relate to others, and make choices in different situations.

During transitional periods, such as moving to a new place, starting university or a new job, going through a breakup or divorce, or experiencing a major life event, mental health can be particularly vulnerable. Coping with change involves adapting to new circumstances, managing uncertainty, and navigating the daunting feelings that often accompany transitions.

Transition phases can lead to a range of emotional and psychological challenges, including stress, anxiety, depression, and difficulty adjusting to new routines and realities. These challenges may stem from feelings of loss, grief, overwhelming expectations, fear of the unknown, a sense of insecurity, or a decrease in social support systems. Therefore, it is essential to prioritize mental health during times of change to ensure a successful transition and overall well-being.

Some strategies for coping with change and maintaining good mental health in transition phases include:

1. Recognizing and accepting emotions:

Acknowledge and validate your feelings during the transition. Understand that it is normal to experience a wide range of emotions, including excitement, fear, sadness, or frustration.

2. Seeking support:

Reach out to friends, family, or mental health professionals who can provide a nurturing and understanding environment. Connecting with others who have experienced similar transitions can be particularly helpful.

3. Establishing a routine:

Create a structured daily routine to establish a sense of stability and control amidst the changes. This can include setting regular sleep patterns, exercise routines, and maintaining a balanced diet.

4. Practicing self-care:

Engage in activities that bring you joy and help you relax. Self-care practices, such as mindfulness, meditation, journaling, or engaging in hobbies, can help reduce stress and promote mental well-being.

5. Taking small steps:

Break down overwhelming tasks or goals into smaller, manageable steps. This can help you feel more accomplished and motivated, reducing feelings of being overwhelmed or stressed.

6. Maintaining a positive mindset:

Challenge negative thoughts by reframing them positively. Focus on the opportunities and growth that can come from the transition rather than dwelling on potential setbacks or difficulties.

7. Seeking professional help if needed:

If you find it difficult to cope with the transition or notice persistent feelings of anxiety or depression, consider seeking support from a mental health professional. They can provide guidance, tools, and therapeutic interventions to support your mental well-being.

Understanding mental health in the context of coping with change during transition phases underscores the importance of self-awareness, self-care, and seeking support. By prioritizing mental health and utilizing effective coping strategies, individuals can navigate life transitions more smoothly and maintain their overall well-being.

3

Importance of Mental Health

In today's fast-paced world, individuals often find themselves navigating through various transitions and changes, which can significantly impact their mental well-being. This overview aims to highlight the importance of mental health in the context of mental health during the transitional phase, specifically focusing on coping with change. It serves as a comprehensive introduction to the subject, shedding light on the challenges faced during transitions and providing insight into maintaining positive mental health.

I. Mental Health and Transitions:

1. Definition:

Mental health refers to a state of emotional, psychological, and social well-being.

2. Transitions:

Transitions encompass significant life changes such as career shifts, relationship changes, moving to a new location, or adjusting to a new life stage.

3. Impact on Mental Health:

MENTAL HEALTH IN THE TRANSITION PHASE: COPING WITH CHANGE

Transitions are often accompanied by stress, anxiety, and uncertainty, which can adversely affect mental health.

II. Coping with Change:

1. Understanding Coping Mechanisms:

Coping refers to the process of managing stress and adapting to change.

2. Common Challenges:

Transitions are frequently associated with challenges like loss, fear, uncertainty, and a sense of being overwhelmed.

3. Coping Strategies:

Effective coping strategies include seeking support, maintaining a healthy lifestyle, practicing mindfulness, learning new skills, and setting realistic goals.

III. Importance of Mental Health in the Transition Phase:

1. Resilience:

A strong mental health foundation can enhance an individual's resilience, enabling them to navigate change more effectively.

2. Emotional Well-being:

Positive mental health facilitates emotional well-being during transitions, promoting a sense of self-worth, optimism, and overall happiness.

3. Productivity and Adaptability:

Good mental health enables individuals to stay focused, manage stress, and adapt to new situations, fostering personal growth and productivity.

IV. Seeking Professional Help:

1. Awareness of Mental Health Issues:

Recognizing signs of mental health challenges during transitions is crucial.

2. Professional Support:

Mental health professionals, such as therapists or counselors, can provide guidance and support to individuals experiencing difficulties during transitions.

3. Importance of Self-Care:

Prioritizing self-care, including engaging in activities that promote relaxation, stress reduction, and self-reflection, can help individuals maintain their mental well-being.

Conclusion:

Understanding the importance of mental health in the context of the subject of mental health in the transition phase: coping with change is necessary to navigate life's challenges successfully. By acknowledging the impact of transitions on mental well-being and employing effective coping strategies, individuals can build resilience and protect their mental health during periods of change. Recognizing the significance of seeking professional help and practicing self-care further contributes to maintaining positive mental health throughout transitional experiences.

4

Common Mental Health Disorders

Mental health is an essential aspect of overall well-being that affects how people think, feel, and act. It encompasses emotional, psychological, and social well-being and plays a significant role in how individuals handle stress, relate to others, and make choices. During transitional phases in life, such as coping with change, mental health can be particularly crucial, as these periods often involve various challenges and adjustments that can impact an individual's mental well-being.

Common Mental Health Disorders:

In the context of mental health during the transition phase, several common mental health disorders can arise. It is essential to understand these conditions in order to recognize their symptoms, seek appropriate support, and promote mental well-being. Here are some of the most prevalent mental health disorders:

1. Generalized Anxiety Disorder (GAD):

GAD is characterized by excessive worry and fear about different aspects of life, accompanied by physical symptoms such as restlessness, difficulty concentrating, and irritability. Transitional phases can heighten anxiety levels due to uncertainties and changes.

2. Major Depressive Disorder (MDD):

MDD involves persistent feelings of sadness, hopelessness, and loss of interest in activities. Coping with significant life changes can trigger or worsen symptoms of depression, making it important to address mental health during such transitions.

3. Post-Traumatic Stress Disorder (PTSD):

PTSD can occur after experiencing or witnessing traumatic events. During transitional phases, individuals may encounter traumatic changes that could trigger symptoms such as flashbacks, nightmares, and hyperarousal.

4. Substance Use Disorders (SUD):

Substance use disorders involve the excessive and problematic use of drugs or alcohol, leading to negative physical, emotional, and social consequences. Transitional phases can be challenging, and some individuals may turn to substance use as a coping mechanism, potentially exacerbating mental health issues.

Coping with Change:

Coping with change during transitional phases is an essential aspect of mental health. Here are some strategies to promote well-being during these periods:

1. Seek Support:

Reach out to friends, family, or professionals to discuss your feelings and concerns. Having a support system in place can provide guidance reassurance, and help in managing change effectively.

2. Maintain Self-Care:

Prioritize self-care activities, such as regular exercise, healthy eating, and sufficient sleep. Engage in hobbies or activities that bring joy and relaxation, allowing for a sense of balance amid transitions.

3. Practice Mindfulness and Stress Reduction Techniques:

Techniques like meditation, deep breathing exercises, and mindfulness can help manage stress, promote self-awareness, and enhance overall well-being.

4. Set Realistic Expectations:

Embrace realistic expectations during transitional phases. Recognize that change takes time and intensity may vary. Be patient with yourself and allow for mistakes and setbacks.

5. Plan and Organize:

Create a plan to navigate the changes ahead, set achievable goals, and break them down into smaller steps. Having a structured approach can alleviate stress and provide a sense of control.

6. Seek Professional Help:

If symptoms worsen or persist, it is essential to consult a mental health professional who can provide guidance and support and potentially recommend therapy or medication if necessary.

Conclusion:

Understanding mental health common disorders in the context of mental health during the transition phase is crucial for promoting well-being and coping effectively with change. By recognizing the signs and symptoms of common mental health disorders, implementing coping strategies, and seeking appropriate support when needed, individuals can navigate transitional phases with resilience and maintain positive mental health.

II

Mental Health During Transition Phases

5

Overview

In the subject of mental health in the transition phase, one important aspect to consider is the impact of change on individuals' mental well-being. Transition phases refer to periods in life when individuals experience significant changes, such as moving to a new city, starting a job or school, ending a relationship, or transitioning into a new life stage. These periods can be challenging and often require individuals to adapt to new situations, environments, and routines, potentially affecting their mental health.

Importance of Mental Health during Transition Phases:

During transition phases, individuals may experience heightened stress, anxiety, and uncertainty as they face the unknown and adjust to new circumstances. Prioritizing mental health during these times becomes crucial as it can influence overall well-being, quality of life, and successful navigation through transitions. Addressing and managing mental health effectively can support individuals in adapting, thriving, and finding happiness during change.

Common Challenges and Coping Strategies:

1. Stress and Anxiety:

Transitions can significantly increase stress and anxiety levels due to the uncertainties and unknowns. Developing stress management techniques, such as deep breathing exercises, mindfulness, and physical activity, can help individuals cope with these challenges.

2. Loss and Grief:

Transition periods often entail losses, such as leaving familiar environments, relationships, or roles behind. Acknowledging and allowing oneself to grieve these losses is essential. Seeking support from loved ones, joining support groups, or seeking counseling can aid in processing these emotions.

3. Identity Formation:

Many transitions involve a reevaluation or transformation of one's identity. Exploring personal values, interests, and strengths can support individuals in fostering a positive sense of self and embracing new identities that align with their transitional phase.

4. Social Support:

Building a strong support network can be beneficial during times of change. Engaging with family, friends, or professional counselors can provide emotional validation, advice, and guidance throughout the transition process.

5. Self-Care:

Engaging in self-care activities, such as maintaining balanced sleep schedules, eating properly, exercising regularly, and practicing relaxation techniques, can significantly contribute to mental well-being during transitions.

6. Seeking Help:

Recognizing when additional support is needed is a sign of strength. Mental health professionals, including therapists, psychologists, or counselors, can offer guidance on coping strategies and provide a space to express emotions during transitional phases.

7. Positive Thinking:

Adopting a positive mindset by reframing challenges as opportunities for growth can help individuals manage stress and uncertainty. Encouraging self-compassion, practicing gratitude, and setting realistic expectations can promote mental well-being during transitions.

Conclusion:

Mental health during transition phases is a critical aspect to consider as individuals navigate through changes in their lives. Developing effective coping strategies can help individuals adapt to new circumstances, manage stress, and maintain overall well-being. By prioritizing mental health and seeking appropriate support, individuals can successfully navigate transition phases, minimizing negative impacts and fostering personal growth and development.

6

Definition of Transition Phase

Transition phases refer to periods of significant change and adaptation in various aspects of one's life. These transitional periods can occur in different contexts, such as personal development, relationships, education, career, and even cultural adjustments. Mental health during transition phases becomes a crucial consideration as these periods often bring about stress, uncertainty, and challenges. Coping with change effectively is essential for maintaining optimal mental well-being during such transitions.

Definition of Transition Phase:

In the context of mental health, a transition phase can be defined as a period marked by substantial shifts or adjustments in one's life circumstances, roles, or identities. These shifts could be planned or unplanned and can lead to changes in physical, emotional, social, or psychological aspects. Transition phases can include various life events such as moving to a new city, starting college, getting married, having a child, career changes, retirement, or bereavement. Each transition phase poses its unique set of challenges and requires individuals to adapt and adjust their mental health strategies accordingly.

Coping with Change:

Coping with change during transition phases is vital to maintaining good mental health. While everyone copes differently, there are some general strategies that can be helpful:

1. Acknowledge and Accept Change:

Recognize that change is a part of life, and accepting it can alleviate distress. Embrace the idea that transitions can present opportunities for growth and self-discovery.

2. Seek Emotional Support:

Reach out to trusted friends, family, or mental health professionals to share your thoughts and emotions and seek guidance. Social support can provide comfort and help develop healthy coping mechanisms.

3. Develop Resilience:

Enhance your ability to bounce back from stressful situations by building resilience. Cultivate self-confidence, positive thinking, and flexibility in adapting to new circumstances.

4. Self-Care and Stress Management:

Prioritize self-care during transition phases by engaging in activities that promote relaxation and well-being. Practice techniques such as exercise, mindfulness, meditation, and sufficient sleep.

5. Set Realistic Goals:

Break down larger tasks into smaller manageable goals. Prioritize and plan action steps to attain these goals, helping create structure and reducing overwhelm.

6. Seek Professional Help:

If the stressors or challenges seem overwhelming, seeking professional help from therapists, counselors, or mental health experts can offer valuable support and guidance.

7. Maintain Healthy Habits:

Focus on maintaining a balanced lifestyle with a healthy diet, regular exercise, and adequate sleep. These foundational aspects of well-being can support mental health during transition phases.

Conclusion:

Mental health during transition phases is critical to successfully navigating life's changes. By recognizing the significance of transition, acknowledging and accepting change, seeking emotional support, developing resilience, practicing self-care, setting realistic goals, and maintaining healthy habits, individuals can cope effectively with the challenges associated with transition phases. Proactive efforts to nurture mental well-being during these times will lead to greater adaptability, growth, and overall improved mental health.

7

Common Transition Phases and Their Impact on Mental Health

Mental health during transition phases is a significant aspect of overall well-being that deserves attention and understanding. Coping with change is a fundamental skill required during these periods, as transitions can greatly impact an individual's mental health. In this overview, we will discuss the concept of mental health during transition phases, common transition phases, and their potential impact on mental health.

1. Definition of Transition Phases:

Transition phases refer to the periods when individuals navigate through significant changes in various aspects of their lives. It can encompass different areas, such as personal, academic, professional, or relationship-oriented transitions. These phases might involve leaving one stage of life and entering a new one, adjusting to new environments, responsibilities, and roles.

2. Mental Health and Transitions:

Mental health plays a crucial role during transition phases. It involves a person's emotional, psychological, and social well-being, affecting how they think, feel, and act. Coping with change is a key component of maintaining positive mental health during transition phases.

3. Common Transition Phases:

a) Childhood to Adolescence: The transition from childhood to adolescence is characterized by physical, emotional, and cognitive changes. Adolescents might experience mood swings, identity exploration, and social pressures, which can impact their mental health.

b) School Transitions: Moving from one educational level to another (e.g., elementary to middle school, high school to college) can be challenging. Students may face academic pressure, peer competition, and the need to adapt to new social environments, which can impact their mental health.

c) Career Transitions: Changing jobs, starting a new profession, or pursuing higher education represents significant changes that can lead to stress, anxiety, and self-doubt. These transitions may evoke concerns about job security, competence, or success, affecting mental well-being.

d) Relationship Transitions: Transitions in relationships, such as marriage, divorce, or becoming a parent, can significantly impact mental health. Adjusting to new dynamics, responsibilities, and emotions can both positively and negatively affect individuals during these phases.

e) Aging and Retirement: Transitioning into older adulthood, retirement, or becoming an empty-nester can have psychological and emotional implications. Individuals may experience feelings of loss and loneliness or find it challenging to adapt to changing roles and routines.

4. Impact on Mental Health:

The impact of transition phases on mental health can vary from person to person. While some individuals might navigate transitions with ease, others may experience heightened levels of stress, anxiety, and depression. Common challenges include adjusting to new routines, managing uncertainty, facing new social dynamics, and dealing with potential loss or grief.

5. Coping with Change:

Developing effective coping mechanisms is vital for maintaining mental health during transition phases. Here are a few strategies individuals can employ:

- Seeking support from family, friends, or professionals, such as counselors or therapists.

- Practicing self-care activities like exercise, meditation, and maintaining a healthy lifestyle.

- Prioritizing open communication and expressing emotions to alleviate stress and anxiety.

- Developing resilience by accepting change, focusing on personal growth, and adapting to new situations.

- Setting realistic goals, breaking tasks into manageable steps, and celebrating achievements along the way.

In conclusion, mental health during transition phases is a crucial aspect of well-being, as change can often impact individuals in significant ways. Understanding the common transition phases and their potential implications on mental health is essential. By adopting effective coping strategies, individuals can successfully navigate through these periods, promoting resilience and overall mental well-being.

8

Specific Mental Health Issues During Transition Phases

Transition phases are periods of significant change that occur throughout our lives. Whether it is transitioning from childhood to adolescence, changing schools, starting a new job, getting married, becoming a parent, or retiring, these transitions can impact our mental health. This overview will explore specific mental health issues that individuals may face during transition phases and delve into coping mechanisms to navigate these changes effectively.

Understanding Transition Phases and Mental Health:

Transition phases involve a disruption in our routine, which can lead to psychological stress and affect our mental well-being. These changes can bring about various mental health issues that individuals might experience.

1. Anxiety and Stress:

Transition phases often encompass uncertainty and alteration of familiar routines, which can trigger anxiety and stress. Individuals may feel overwhelmed, experience difficulties in decision-making, and face worries about the future.

SPECIFIC MENTAL HEALTH ISSUES DURING TRANSITION PHASES

2. Depression and Sadness:

Psychological distress and loneliness may arise during transition phases, leading to feelings of sadness and even depression. Disconnection from previous support systems, loss of identity, or struggles to adapt to new environments can contribute to these emotions.

3. Self-Identity and Self-Esteem:

Transitions often challenge individuals' sense of identity and confidence. Adjusting to new roles, responsibilities, or environments can cause individuals to question their self-worth, leading to diminished self-esteem and potential identity crises.

4. Social Isolation:

Transition phases may result in individuals feeling alienated or disconnected from their social networks. Relocation, changing social circles, or starting a new phase of education or career can leave individuals feeling isolated and lacking supportive relationships.

Coping Strategies:

To maintain positive mental health during transition phases, there are several coping strategies individuals can employ:

1. Seek Support:

Engage with friends, family, or support groups who can offer guidance, empathy, and reassurance during this period of change.

2. Maintain a Routine:

Establishing a structured routine can provide a sense of stability and familiarity, easing the transition process.

3. Practice Self-Care:

Focus on activities that promote mental well-being, such as exercise, meditation, hobbies, relaxation techniques, and taking breaks when needed.

4. Set Realistic Goals:

Break down larger goals into smaller, achievable tasks to maintain motivation and reduce feelings of being overwhelmed.

5. Be Flexible and Embrace Change:

Develop a growth mindset and view transitions as opportunities for personal growth and development. Embrace change, adapt to new circumstances, and capitalize on the potential for positive change.

6. Seek Professional Help:

If mental health issues become overwhelming or persistent during transition phases, seeking professional help from therapists or counselors can provide valuable guidance and support.

Conclusion:

Transition phases can challenge our mental health and well-being due to their disruptive nature. However, by recognizing the potential mental health issues that may arise and implementing coping strategies, individuals can navigate change successfully. By seeking support, cultivating a positive mindset, maintaining self-care practices, and embracing change, individuals can promote their mental health and resilience during these transition phases.

III

Coping with Change

9

Overview

Coping with change is an essential aspect of navigating through life's transitions, particularly during the transition phase when individuals experience significant shifts in their personal, academic, or professional lives. Changes can range from moving to a new city, entering a new school or workplace, starting or ending relationships, or even experiencing major life events such as marriage, parenthood, or retirement. In the context of mental health, coping with change requires individuals to adapt and manage their emotions, behaviors, and thoughts effectively. This overview explores the impact of change on mental health during the transition phase, identifies common challenges faced, and provides practical coping strategies.

Impact of Change on Mental Health:

The transition phase can sometimes be overwhelming, leading to various mental health challenges such as increased stress, anxiety, depression, and even a sense of loss. Change can disrupt established routines, expose individuals to unfamiliar situations, and trigger feelings of uncertainty, fear, or isolation. The pressure to adapt quickly and successfully can also contribute to mental health difficulties. It is essential to recognize that everyone's response to change is unique, and individuals may experience a wide range of emotional and psychological reactions.

MENTAL HEALTH IN THE TRANSITION PHASE: COPING WITH CHANGE

Common Challenges Faced:

1. Uncertainty:

Change often brings uncertainty as individuals step into unfamiliar territories. This uncertainty can create feelings of insecurity and make it challenging to make decisions or plan for the future.

2. Loss and grief:

Transition periods often involve leaving behind familiar environments, relationships, or experiences, which can provoke feelings of loss and grief.

3. Increased stress:

The added responsibilities and demands that come with change can lead to heightened levels of stress. This stress can impact various aspects of life, including relationships, work or school performance, and physical well-being.

4. Self-doubt and fear:

Change can sometimes trigger self-doubt and fears about one's abilities to adapt, succeed, or handle new challenges. This can impact self-esteem and confidence levels.

5. Social isolation:

Entering new environments or leaving familiar ones can also result in a sense of isolation or disconnection from support networks, which can negatively affect mental well-being.

Coping Strategies:

OVERVIEW

1. Self-care:

Prioritize self-care activities such as exercise, adequate sleep, healthy eating, and engaging in activities that bring joy and relaxation. Taking care of physical health can positively impact mental well-being.

2. Establish a routine:

Creating a new routine, whether it's related to work, study, or personal life, can provide a sense of structure and stability during times of change.

3. Seek support:

Reach out to friends, family, or professionals who can provide emotional support. Sharing concerns, fears, and uncertainties with trusted individuals can alleviate emotional burdens.

4. Practice mindfulness and stress-reducing techniques:

Engaging in mindfulness meditation, deep breathing exercises, or other stress-reduction techniques can help manage anxiety and increase resilience.

5. Set realistic expectations:

Recognize that it's normal to experience various emotions during periods of change. Accept and validate your feelings, and avoid putting unrealistic pressure on yourself to adapt flawlessly or immediately.

6. Focus on the positive:

Instead of dwelling on what is lost or uncertain, redirect your attention towards the positive aspects of the change. Reflect on the potential opportunities, personal growth, or new experiences that may arise from the transition.

7. Seek professional help if needed:

If coping with change becomes overwhelming and starts significantly impacting mental health or daily functioning, it is advisable to seek the guidance of a mental health professional who can provide tailored support and coping strategies.

Conclusion:

Coping with change during the transition phase is essential for maintaining good mental health. Understanding the impact of change, identifying common challenges, and implementing effective coping strategies can help individuals successfully navigate through periods of transition. Remember that change is a constant part of life, and with the right mindset and support, it can be a catalyst for personal growth, resilience, and new opportunities.

10

Understanding Change

Change is an inevitable part of life, and navigating through changes can be challenging, particularly in the transition phase. This period encompasses various life transitions like relocating to a new place, starting a new job, transitioning to parenthood, or adjusting to changes in relationships. In the context of mental health, coping with change becomes crucial as it can impact individuals' well-being and overall psychological state. This overview aims to provide a comprehensive understanding of coping with change in the transition phase, focusing on mental health.

Understanding Change:

Change can be defined as any alteration in one's environment, circumstances, relationships, or routine. It can be both anticipated and unexpected, requiring individuals to adapt and adjust their behavior, thoughts, and emotions accordingly. In the transition phase, change often brings a sense of uncertainty and can evoke mixed emotions, such as excitement, fear, and anxiety.

Coping Strategies:

1. Recognizing and Accepting Change:

Acknowledging that change is a natural part of life helps in accepting it rather than resisting it. Understanding that change can offer new opportunities and growth can be empowering.

2. Building Resilience:

Resilience refers to one's ability to bounce back from adversity. Developing resilience can be beneficial for coping with change as it enables individuals to adapt and adjust more effectively. This can be achieved through enhancing problem-solving skills, fostering positive thinking, and maintaining a support system.

3. Developing Self-awareness:

Being aware of one's strengths, weaknesses, values, and interests can help individuals make conscious choices during the transition phase. Self-awareness enables individuals to align their goals and values with the changes they are experiencing, promoting a smoother transition.

4. Seeking Support:

Seeking support from friends, family, or professionals can be immensely helpful when coping with change. Connecting with others who have experienced similar transitions can provide valuable insights, guidance, validation, and emotional support.

5. Managing Stress:

Change can often be accompanied by increased stress levels. Implementing stress management techniques such as exercise, relaxation exercises, and mindfulness can help reduce anxiety and promote overall well-being.

Impact on Mental Health:

Navigating through significant changes during the transition phase can have both positive and negative impacts on mental health. Positive changes can enhance self-esteem, happiness, and personal growth. Conversely, major life changes can also trigger stress, anxiety, depression, and feelings of loss or grief. It is crucial to be aware of the potential impact on mental health and take preventive measures to maintain well-being.

Conclusion:

Coping with change in the transition phase has a significant impact on mental health. It is essential to develop effective coping strategies, recognize and accept change, build resilience, seek support, and manage stress to navigate through these transitions successfully. By understanding the challenges associated with change, individuals can promote their mental well-being and embrace the opportunities that change brings.

11

The Psychological Impact of Change

In life, change is inevitable. Whether it is a transition to a new job, a move to a different city, or a major life event, change can have a profound impact on our mental health and well-being. Coping with change is a crucial skill that allows individuals to navigate through these transitions effectively. This overview will explore the psychological impact of change, particularly in the context of mental health during the transition phase.

Understanding the Transition Phase:

The transition phase refers to a period in which individuals experience a significant change in their circumstances, routines, or roles. It could be a developmental transition such as entering adulthood, transitioning to a new career, or a life event like getting married or becoming a parent. This phase often comes with a mix of excitement, uncertainty, and stress, triggering various psychological responses.

Psychological Impact of Change:

1. Stress and Anxiety:

Change can be accompanied by heightened levels of stress and anxiety.

Uncertainty about the future, fear of the unknown, and a perceived loss of control can all contribute to these feelings. Individuals may experience symptoms such as restlessness, irritability, difficulty sleeping, or racing thoughts.

2. Loss and Grief:

Even positive changes can bring about a sense of loss for the familiar or the previous situation. For example, leaving behind friends and connections when moving to a new place. These losses can lead to feelings of grief, sadness, and nostalgia. It is important to acknowledge and process these emotions to facilitate healthy coping.

3. Identity and Self-esteem:

Change often requires individuals to adapt and adjust their sense of self and identity. This process can challenge one's self-esteem, as individuals may question their abilities and competence in the new context. Developing a resilient mindset and seeking support from others can help in maintaining and rebuilding a positive self-image.

4. Uncertainty and Fear:

Change often involves stepping into the unknown, which can evoke a sense of uncertainty and fear. Some individuals may be resistant to change due to a fear of failure or the unfamiliar. Building resilience, practicing self-compassion, and reframing perspectives can aid in addressing these fears.

Coping with Change:

1. Acceptance and Adaptation:

Recognizing and accepting that change is a normal part of life is crucial.

Embracing flexibility and adaptability can help individuals navigate through transitions more effectively. This involves reframing change as an opportunity for growth and personal development rather than a threat.

2. Seeking Support:

It is essential to reach out to friends, family, or mental health professionals for support during times of change. Building a strong support system can offer guidance, comfort, and encouragement. Therapeutic interventions such as counseling or therapy can also assist in processing emotions and developing effective coping strategies.

3. Self-care and Stress Management:

Engaging in self-care activities can help individuals reduce stress and enhance their emotional well-being during times of change. This includes practicing mindfulness, maintaining a healthy lifestyle, engaging in hobbies, and setting boundaries to manage stress effectively.

4. Building Resilience:

Resilience is the ability to bounce back from adversity, and it plays a vital role in coping with change. Developing resilience involves cultivating optimism, problem-solving skills, and enhancing emotional regulation. Self-reflection and learning from past experiences can also contribute to building resilience.

Conclusion:

Coping with change during the transition phase is a critical aspect of maintaining mental health and well-being. By understanding the psychological impact of change and employing effective coping strategies, individuals can navigate through life's transitions more smoothly. Seeking support, promoting resilience, and practicing self-care are essential tools for coping with change and fostering personal growth in the face of new challenges.

12

Strategies for Coping with Change

Coping with change is an essential skill for maintaining good mental health, particularly during transitional phases. Whether it's switching careers, moving to a new city, or experiencing major life events, individuals often encounter feelings of uncertainty, stress, and anxiety. This overview will explore effective strategies for coping with change in the context of mental health during transitional phases.

Understanding Coping with Change:

Coping with change refers to the adaptive processes individuals engage in to manage and navigate the challenges associated with significant life transitions. It involves developing resilience, emotional regulation, and problem-solving skills. Coping strategies can support individuals in maintaining mental well-being and adapting successfully to new circumstances.

Essential Coping Strategies:

1. Acceptance:

Recognize that change is a natural part of life and accept that it may involve both positive and negative aspects. Adopting a mindset of acceptance can reduce resistance and facilitate the adjustment process.

2. Self-care:

Prioritizing self-care activities such as exercise, maintaining a balanced diet, getting enough sleep, and engaging in relaxation techniques like meditation and deep breathing can help manage stress and promote mental well-being.

3. Seek support:

Reach out to friends, family, or support groups who can provide guidance, reassurance, and empathy during the transition phase. Professional mental health support, such as therapy or counseling services, can also be beneficial.

4. Develop a routine:

Establishing a structured daily routine can provide a sense of stability during times of change. Having a predictable schedule helps individuals feel more organized and grounded.

5. Emotional expression:

Allow yourself to experience and express your emotions. Whether through journaling, talking to a trusted confidant, or art therapies, expressing emotions can help you process and accept the changes happening in your life.

6. Cognitive reframing:

Reframing negative thoughts into more positive and realistic perspectives can minimize distress. Challenge negative beliefs by examining evidence and considering alternative explanations or possibilities.

7. Set realistic goals:

Break down larger tasks into smaller, achievable goals. This approach not only provides a sense of accomplishment but also reduces feelings of overwhelm often associated with major life changes.

8. Maintain healthy boundaries:

Clearly define boundaries and communicate them effectively with others. Protect your time, energy, and overall well-being by being mindful of unhealthy dynamics in relationships.

9. Embrace uncertainty:

Uncertainty is often an inherent part of change. Develop a flexible mindset and practice embracing the unknown. Focus on adapting, growing, and learning from new experiences.

10. Patience and self-compassion:

Remember that adjusting to change takes time. Be patient with yourself and avoid self-judgment or excessive self-criticism. Embrace self-compassion and treat yourself with kindness throughout the transition phase.

Conclusion:

Coping with change during transitional phases is crucial for maintaining mental health. By integrating strategies such as acceptance, self-care, seeking support, and developing a routine, individuals can effectively manage stress, adapt to new circumstances, and foster personal growth. Through employing healthy coping mechanisms, it becomes possible to navigate the complexities of change with resilience and greater well-being.

IV

Mental Health Care

13

Overview

Mental health care in the context of the subject of mental health in the transition phase, coping with change, plays a crucial role in supporting individuals during times of transition and helping them cope with the challenges and stress that these periods may bring. Transition phases can occur in various aspects of life, such as transitioning from adolescence to adulthood, changing careers, entering or leaving a relationship, or any significant life event that requires adjustment to new circumstances.

During these transitions, individuals may experience a range of emotions, including anxiety, stress, confusion, and even depression. Mental health care aims to provide support, guidance, and resources to individuals to help them navigate through these changes in a healthy and productive way.

One key aspect of mental health care in the context of transition is the recognition and validation of the individual's emotions and experiences. Transitions can be challenging, and individuals may feel a sense of loss, uncertainty, or fear. Mental health care professionals, such as therapists, counselors, or psychologists, provide a safe and non-judgmental space for individuals to express their feelings and explore their concerns.

Another important role of mental health care in the context of transition is to help individuals develop coping mechanisms and adaptive strategies. This involves helping individuals identify their strengths, build resilience, and learn effective ways to manage stress and anxiety. Mental health care professionals may employ techniques such as cognitive-behavioral therapy, mindfulness practices, or other evidence-based interventions to assist individuals in developing these skills.

In addition to individual therapy, mental health care in transition phases may also involve group therapy or support groups. These group settings provide individuals with the opportunity to connect with others going through similar experiences, share their stories, and learn from one another. Group therapy can be especially beneficial for individuals who feel isolated or lonely during transitional periods.

Furthermore, mental health care in the context of transition emphasizes the importance of self-care and self-compassion. Transition phases can be demanding and overwhelming, and individuals may neglect their physical and emotional well-being. Mental health care professionals may help individuals prioritize self-care practices such as exercise, healthy eating, quality sleep, and engaging in activities they enjoy. Additionally, individuals are encouraged to be kind and compassionate towards themselves, practicing self-acceptance and acknowledging that it is okay to seek support during challenging times.

It is important to note that mental health care during transition phases is not limited to professional interventions. Friends, family, and support networks also play an essential role in providing emotional support and understanding. Mental health care professionals may collaborate with these networks to create a comprehensive support system for individuals undergoing transitions.

In summary, mental health care in the context of mental health in the transition phase, coping with change, aims to support individuals during periods of transition by validating their emotions, helping them develop coping mechanisms, fostering connections through group therapy or support groups, promoting self-care and self-compassion, and collaborating with support networks. By providing such comprehensive care, mental health professionals empower individuals to navigate through transitions successfully and enhance their overall well-being.

14

The Role of Professional Help in Mental Health Care

In the context of mental health in the transition phase, coping with change plays a crucial role in maintaining one's mental well-being. Change is an inevitable part of life, and during transitional periods, such as moving to a new city, starting college, or changing careers, individuals may experience increased stress and psychological challenges. Professional help in mental health care plays a vital role in providing support, guidance, and treatment strategies to help individuals navigate these changes effectively.

Mental health care encompasses a wide range of services aimed at promoting psychological well-being, preventing mental disorders, and treating existing mental health conditions. Professional help is offered by trained experts, such as psychologists, therapists, psychiatrists, and counselors, who possess the knowledge, skills, and experience to address various mental health concerns.

During transitional phases, individuals may experience a range of emotional difficulties, including anxiety, depression, stress, and uncertainty. Professional help offers a safe and confidential space for individuals to explore their feelings, thoughts, and concerns associated with these changes. Therapeutic interventions, such as cognitive-behavioral therapy (CBT), dialectical behavior therapy (DBT), or psychodynamic therapy, can be employed to assist individuals in developing coping strategies specific to their needs.

The role of professional help in mental health care during transition is multi-fold. Firstly, professionals assess individuals' mental health status by conducting diagnostic evaluations and clinical assessments. Through these evaluations, professionals can identify potential mental health disorders, evaluate the severity of symptoms, and determine appropriate treatment approaches.

Secondly, mental health professionals provide psychoeducation, equipping individuals with knowledge about mental health, stress management, and healthy coping mechanisms. This helps individuals understand their emotions and develop self-awareness, enabling them to make informed decisions regarding their mental well-being.

Thirdly, professionals offer evidence-based interventions tailored to individual needs. These interventions may include individual therapy, group therapy, family therapy, or medication management when necessary. Through therapeutic sessions, professionals help individuals develop healthier thinking patterns, build resilience, foster emotional regulation, and improve interpersonal skills to cope with the challenges of transition.

Moreover, professionals provide support in crisis situations. They are trained in identifying and managing mental health emergencies, such as suicidal ideation or severe anxiety attacks.

In addition to direct intervention, mental health professionals collaborate with other healthcare providers, such as primary care physicians or social workers, to ensure comprehensive and holistic care. They may also refer individuals to other specialized services, such as support groups, rehabilitation programs, or community resources that can be beneficial during the transition phase.

It is important to note that seeking professional help is not indicative of weakness but rather a proactive step towards prioritizing mental well-being. It offers individuals an opportunity to address their mental health concerns in a timely manner, preventing potential complications and empowering them to adapt to and cope with change effectively.

In conclusion, professional help in mental health care plays a significant role in supporting individuals during transitional phases and coping with change. By providing assessment, psychoeducation, evidence-based interventions, crisis support, and collaboration with other healthcare providers, mental health professionals contribute to the overall mental well-being of individuals as they navigate the challenges of transition. Seeking professional help offers a valuable resource for individuals to develop resilience, enhance coping strategies, and thrive during periods of change.

15

Self-care Strategies for Mental Health

Mental health care self-care strategies are an essential component of maintaining good mental well-being, especially during times of transition or change. The transition phase refers to periods in life when individuals experience significant shifts in their circumstances, such as starting college, changing jobs, moving to a new city, or going through a major life event.

Coping with change can be challenging and may impact one's mental health. Therefore, it is important to develop self-care strategies that promote emotional resilience and psychological well-being during such transitional phases. Here is an extensive overview of self-care strategies for mental health in the context of coping with change:

1. Establish a Support Network:

Build a strong support system by connecting with friends, family, mentors, or support groups who can provide guidance, understanding, and encouragement. Talking to someone who has gone through a similar transition can be particularly helpful.

2. Maintain Healthy Relationships:

Nourish existing relationships and cultivate new ones to combat feelings of isolation and loneliness. Prioritize spending time with loved ones and engage in activities that promote mutual enjoyment and support.

3. Practice Relaxation Techniques:

Incorporate stress-reduction techniques into your routine. Deep breathing exercises, meditation, yoga, or mindfulness can help calm the mind, reduce anxiety, and increase self-awareness.

4. Prioritize Sleep:

Establish a consistent sleep schedule and create a sleep-friendly environment. Aim for 7-9 hours of quality sleep each night, as it positively impacts mood, cognition, and overall well-being.

5. Exercise Regularly:

Engage in physical activities that you enjoy, such as walking, jogging, swimming, or dancing. Regular exercise releases endorphins, which are natural mood enhancers, and helps reduce stress and anxiety.

6. Maintain a Balanced Diet:

Nutritional choices can influence mental health. Ensure you consume a well-balanced diet rich in fruits, vegetables, whole grains, lean proteins, and healthy fats. Avoid excessive caffeine, sugary foods, and processed snacks, as they can negatively affect mood and energy levels.

7. Set Realistic Goals:

Break down larger tasks into smaller achievable goals. This helps maintain motivation, fosters a sense of accomplishment, and reduces feelings of being overwhelmed.

8. Engage in Activities You Enjoy:

Allocate time for hobbies, leisure activities, and interests that bring you joy and relaxation. Engaging in activities you enjoy can help reduce stress and promote positive emotions.

9. Seek Professional Help:

If you find yourself struggling to cope with the transition or experiencing persistent mental health challenges, seek support from mental health professionals. They can provide guidance, therapy, or appropriate interventions tailored to your individual needs.

10. Practice Self-Compassion:

Be kind to yourself during the transition phase. Acknowledge that it is normal to experience a range of emotions and setbacks. Treat yourself with compassion, practice positive self-talk, and focus on personal growth rather than perfection.

Remember, self-care should be personalized and adapted to meet your unique needs and circumstances. Experiment with different strategies and identify what works best for you. Taking care of your mental health during times of change is essential to navigate transitions successfully and maintain overall well-being.

16

The Importance of Social Support in Mental Health Care

Mental health care plays a crucial role in helping individuals navigate the challenges they face during the transition phase of their lives. The transition phase refers to periods of significant change, such as moving to a new city, starting a new job, getting married, or entering retirement. These life transitions can often be stressful and overwhelming, leading to mental health issues if not properly addressed.

In the context of mental health care during the transition phase, social support plays a vital role. Social support refers to the assistance and resources that individuals receive from their social networks, including family, friends, colleagues, and community members. The presence of a strong support system can significantly impact an individual's ability to cope with change and maintain good mental health.

Importance of Social Support:

1. Emotional Support:

During times of transition, individuals may experience a wide range of emotions, including stress, anxiety, sadness, or uncertainty. Having a strong social support network can provide emotional comfort and understanding. Friends and family can offer a listening ear, empathy, and validation, which can help alleviate mental health issues.

2. Practical Support:

Social support helps individuals manage the practical challenges that often arise during transitions. For instance, friends or family members can assist with logistical tasks like packing, moving, or providing child care. This practical assistance can help reduce stress and free up mental energy that can be directed towards adjusting to the change.

3. Informational Support:

Social networks can serve as valuable sources of information and guidance during transitions. Friends or colleagues who have gone through similar experiences can share insights, advice, and resources to help individuals better understand and navigate the changes they are facing. This knowledge can enhance problem-solving skills and increase feelings of control and competence.

4. Social Integration:

Building new social connections and networks is particularly important during the transition phase. Social support can provide opportunities for social integration by introducing individuals to new friendships, professional networks, or community groups. These connections can foster a sense of belonging, reduce feelings of isolation, and promote overall mental well-being.

5. Alleviating Stigma:

Mental health issues often carry a social stigma that may prevent individuals from seeking help. However, strong social support systems can help reduce the stigma associated with mental health challenges by providing acceptance, understanding, and encouragement. This can create a safe space for individuals to openly discuss their mental health concerns and seek appropriate professional help if needed.

Overall, social support is a fundamental component of mental health care during the transition phase. It facilitates emotional well-being, enhances coping mechanisms, and promotes resilience in times of change. Recognizing the importance of social support and actively seeking it out can significantly contribute to an individual's ability to adapt and thrive during life transitions.

V

Future Research Directions

17

Overview

The transition phase is a critical period in a person's life when they experience significant changes in various domains, such as education, employment, relationships, and identity development. These changes can lead to significant stress, which in turn affects mental health outcomes. Understanding and addressing mental health during this transition phase is crucial for promoting positive psychological well-being and preventing the onset of mental disorders. Therefore, future research directions in the context of mental health in the transition phase primarily focus on identifying effective strategies to cope with change and enhance mental well-being.

1. Identification of Risk Factors:

Future research should aim to identify specific risk factors that make individuals more vulnerable to mental health challenges during the transition phase. For instance, investigating the influence of pre-existing mental health conditions, socioeconomic status, cultural factors, and personal characteristics on mental health outcomes can help develop targeted interventions.

2. Development of Intervention Programs:

Effective intervention programs tailored to the transition period are needed to promote mental health and well-being. Research should focus on developing evidence-based interventions that address common mental health challenges during this phase, such as anxiety, depression, and stress. These programs may involve cognitive-behavioral therapy, mindfulness-based practices, psychoeducation, and support groups.

3. Technology-Mediated Interventions:

Integrating technology into mental health interventions can provide accessible and cost-effective solutions for young adults going through transitional phases. Future research should explore the use of mobile applications, online platforms, virtual reality, and wearable devices to deliver interventions, monitor mental health outcomes, and provide timely support and resources.

4. Resilience and Self-Efficacy Promotion:

Research should delve into factors promoting resilience and self-efficacy during the transition phase. Understanding the protective factors that contribute to positive mental health outcomes, such as social support, coping mechanisms, and self-beliefs, can aid in developing interventions that bolster these factors and promote individuals' ability to adapt to change successfully.

5. Longitudinal Studies:

Conducting longitudinal studies that follow individuals over an extended period can provide valuable insights into the long-term consequences of mental health challenges in the transition phase. Such research can uncover the impact of unresolved mental health issues during this time on later stages of life and help develop preventative strategies.

6. Cultural and Contextual Influences:

It is vital to account for cultural and contextual influences on mental health outcomes during the transition phase. Future research should investigate how different cultural norms, societal expectations, and the availability of resources impact mental health and coping mechanisms. This understanding can inform the development of culturally sensitive interventions.

7. Implementation and Dissemination of Findings:

Once effective interventions are developed, research should focus on methods to implement and disseminate these programs on a larger scale. This may involve collaboration with educational institutions, healthcare providers, community organizations, and policymakers to ensure widespread access and utilization of evidence-based interventions.

In conclusion, future research directions in the context of mental health in the transition phase aim to identify risk factors, develop intervention programs, explore technology-mediated solutions, promote resilience, conduct longitudinal studies, consider cultural influences, and ensure the implementation and dissemination of findings. By addressing mental health challenges during this critical period, individuals can effectively cope with changes, enhance their well-being, and minimize the risk of mental health disorders.

18

Current Gaps in Mental Health Research

Mental health plays a crucial role in an individual's ability to navigate through life's transitions, especially during periods of significant change. The transition phase includes events such as adolescence, entering college or the workforce, marriage or divorce, parenthood, and retirement, all of which can bring about various challenges and stressors. Understanding and addressing mental health concerns during these transitional phases is vital for promoting overall well-being. This article provides an extensive overview of future research directions and current gaps in mental health research specifically focused on coping with change.

1. Identify and Define Key Mental Health Challenges in Transition Phases:

A significant research direction would involve the identification and definition of specific mental health challenges that individuals commonly face during transition phases. These could encompass issues related to identity formation, self-esteem, anxiety, depression, stress, and social support. Research should aim to elucidate the unique characteristics and risk factors associated with mental health during these periods.

2. Identify Protective Factors and Resilience-building Strategies:

Focusing on the identification and exploration of protective factors and resilience-building strategies would be crucial. Investigating factors such as social support, coping mechanisms, mindfulness practices, and other positive psychological resources can highlight potential interventions that promote mental well-being during transitions.

3. Develop Targeted Interventions:

Future research should concentrate on developing and evaluating targeted interventions that address mental health concerns during specific transition phases. For example, interventions designed for adolescents may differ from those aimed at supporting older adults. Identifying effective intervention strategies and evaluating their long-term impact on mental health outcomes is essential.

4. Explore the Role of Technology:

Considering the increasing reliance on technology in modern life, investigating the impact of digital tools on mental health during transitions is essential. Research should explore how technology can be utilized to provide support, promote resilience, and enhance mental health outcomes. This includes examining the efficacy of digital platforms, mobile applications, and wearable devices as potential sources of mental health support.

5. Address Cultural and Societal Factors:

Mental health research must acknowledge and address cultural and societal factors that influence the experience of coping with change. Research should focus on understanding how factors such as cultural norms, social expectations, and community support systems impact mental health outcomes during transition phases. This knowledge can inform the development of culturally sensitive interventions.

6. Longitudinal Studies:

Conducting longitudinal studies that follow individuals over an extended period through different transition phases is crucial for understanding the long-term impact of transition-related mental health concerns. Examining trajectories of mental health, identifying risk factors, and evaluating the effects of various interventions can provide valuable insights into effective strategies for promoting mental well-being.

Conclusion:

Future research in the field of mental health during transition phases requires a comprehensive approach encompassing the identification of key challenges, exploration of protective factors, targeted interventions, investigation of technology, consideration of cultural factors, and longitudinal studies. Addressing these research directions and filling the current gaps can facilitate the development of evidence-based interventions and support systems to enhance mental health outcomes during periods of change.

19

Future Research Opportunities in Mental Health

Future research directions and opportunities in mental health, specifically focusing on the transition phase of coping with change, hold immense potential for improving our understanding and treatment of mental health issues during this critical period of life. This overview will highlight some key areas that researchers can explore to contribute to the field and address the challenges individuals face when transitioning through various life changes.

1. Longitudinal studies:

Conducting extensive longitudinal studies can provide valuable insights into mental health trajectories during the transition phase. Researchers can track individuals over time and examine the factors that influence their coping mechanisms, resilience, and vulnerability to mental health issues. Understanding the long-term impacts of mental health challenges during transitions is crucial for developing effective interventions.

2. Protective factors and resilience:

Exploring the protective factors that promote resilience and positive mental health outcomes in the face of change is essential. Identifying individual, social, and environmental factors that contribute to successful coping can help develop targeted interventions and support systems for those who struggle during transitions.

3. Technology-based interventions:

The integration of technology in mental health research and interventions offers vast opportunities. Investigating the effectiveness of digital interventions, mobile applications, virtual reality, and other technology-based tools can enhance accessibility, effectiveness, and customization of mental health support during transition periods.

4. Cultural and societal factors:

Examining how cultural and societal norms impact mental health in the context of transitioning is crucial. Research can focus on understanding differential experiences and developing culturally sensitive interventions that consider factors such as family support, social norms, beliefs, and values that influence mental health outcomes.

5. Identification of high-risk groups:

Identifying specific populations or groups that experience higher rates of mental health issues during transitions is essential for targeted intervention. Research can focus on specific demographics, such as young adults, immigrants, LGBTQ+ individuals, or individuals with chronic illnesses, to explore the unique challenges and develop appropriate support systems.

6. Prevention and early intervention:

Developing effective prevention and early intervention strategies can mitigate the negative impact of mental health issues during transitions. Research can focus on identifying early warning signs, implementing screening tools, and designing interventions that empower individuals to proactively manage their mental health during times of change.

7. Integrated care approaches:

Exploring integrated care models that bridge mental health and other related disciplines can enhance holistic support during transitions. Collaboration between mental health specialists, primary care providers, educators, and community organizations can create comprehensive systems that address the unique needs of individuals navigating periods of change.

8. Stigma reduction:

Investigating strategies to reduce stigma surrounding mental health during transitions is crucial for fostering a supportive environment. Research can focus on developing educational programs, media campaigns, and community initiatives that promote understanding, acceptance, and empathy for individuals experiencing mental health challenges.

9. Intersectionality:

Recognizing the intersectionality of various identities, such as gender, race, socioeconomic status, and disability, is imperative in understanding mental health experiences during transitions comprehensively. Research that acknowledges and incorporates intersectional perspectives can lead to more inclusive interventions and policy recommendations.

10. Global perspectives:

Exploring mental health in the context of the transition phase from a global perspective can provide insights into how different cultures and societies approach and address these challenges. Comparative research can facilitate sharing of best practices and mutual learning to improve mental health outcomes worldwide.

In conclusion, future research directions and opportunities in mental health within the transition phase of coping with change offer significant potential for advancing our understanding and support for individuals. By focusing on longitudinal studies, protective factors, technology-based interventions, cultural influences, high-risk groups, prevention, integrated care, stigma reduction, intersectionality, and global perspectives, researchers can contribute to the development of effective interventions and policies that enhance mental health during periods of change.

20

The Potential Impact of Future Mental Health Research.

The field of mental health research is constantly evolving, and there are several future research directions that show great potential in understanding and addressing mental health issues, particularly in the context of the transition phase and coping with change. This overview will highlight some of these directions and the potential impact they could have on individuals and society at large.

1. Neurobiology of resilience:

Resilience refers to an individual's ability to cope with stress and bounce back from adversity. Future research in this area aims to explore the underlying neurobiological mechanisms that contribute to resilience, which could lead to the development of targeted interventions to enhance resilience and improve mental well-being during times of transition and change.

2. Personalized interventions:

Advances in technology and data analysis have enabled the development of personalized approaches to mental health interventions. Future research may focus on leveraging various data sources, such as genetic information, biomarkers, or behavioral patterns, to tailor interventions to an individual's specific needs and circumstances. Personalized interventions have the potential to optimize treatment outcomes and improve psychological outcomes during transitions.

3. Prevention and early intervention:

Identifying individuals at risk for mental health problems early on and providing timely interventions can have a profound impact on their outcomes. Future research may explore novel strategies for early detection and prevention of mental health conditions during the transition phase. This could involve the development and testing of screening tools, as well as the implementation and evaluation of early intervention programs in educational or workplace settings.

4. Technology and digital mental health interventions:

The use of technology, such as mobile apps, virtual reality, and online platforms, has revolutionized mental health care delivery. Future research may delve into the efficacy, accessibility, and cost-effectiveness of these digital interventions, specifically tailored to individuals navigating through transitions and coping with change. Additionally, the ethical considerations and potential drawbacks of the widespread adoption of technology in mental health care would also be important areas of investigation.

5. Intersectionality and cultural factors:

Mental health experiences and needs vary across different cultures, communities, and identities. Future research could explore the intersectionality of mental health, considering factors such as ethnicity, gender, socioeconomic status, and sexual orientation to better understand how these factors influence mental health outcomes during the transition phase. This research can help identify disparities in access to mental health care and inform the development of culturally sensitive interventions.

6. Stigma reduction and public awareness:

Despite advancements in research and treatment options, mental health stigma remains a significant barrier to seeking help and support. Future research may focus on strategies to reduce stigma, increase public awareness, and normalize conversations surrounding mental health during times of transition. This could involve community-based interventions, educational campaigns, and policy changes aimed at promoting mental well-being.

In conclusion, future mental health research in the context of the transition phase and coping with change holds immense promise. The potential impacts range from identifying the neural basis of resilience to providing personalized interventions, enabling prevention and early intervention, leveraging technology for digital mental health care, and addressing cultural and intersectional factors. By continuing to advance knowledge in these areas, we can strive towards a future where mental health is better understood, adequately supported, and successfully navigated during times of transition.

About the Author

Sophia Newleaf is a celebrated psychologist and thought leader in the realm of personal growth and adaptability. With over two decades of experience, she has guided countless individuals through life's most challenging transitions, helping them find balance, purpose, and resilience.

Sophia's approach is rooted in a blend of evidence-based practices and holistic well-being. Her personal journey through significant life changes has not only shaped her professional trajectory but also deepened her understanding of the emotional complexities individuals face during transitions.

A sought-after speaker and workshop facilitator, Sophia's insights have been featured in numerous publications and platforms. Beyond her professional accolades, she is passionate about nature, mindfulness practices, and the art of storytelling.

In "Mental Health in the Transition Phase," Sophia brings together her vast expertise and personal experiences, offering readers a compassionate guide to navigating change with grace and confidence.

This "About the Author" section aims to establish Sophia Newleaf's expertise, experience, and personal connection to the topic, making her a trustworthy guide for readers.

www.ingramcontent.com/pod-product-compliance
Lightning Source LLC
Chambersburg PA
CBHW031301290426
44109CB00012B/675